ALASKA GEOGRAPHIC

Volume 16, Number 1

Katmai Country

The Alaska Geographic Society

To teach many more to better know and use our natural resources

Editor: Penny Rennick
Associate Editor: Kathy Doogan
Creative Director: Don Schnabel
Designer: Sandra Harner

ALASKA GEOGRAPHIC®, ISSN 0361-1353, is published quarterly by The Alaska Geographic Society, Anchorage, Alaska 99509-3370. Second-class postage paid in Edmonds, Washington 98020-3512. Printed in U.S.A. Copyright © 1989 by The Alaska Geographic Society. All rights reserved. Registered trademark; Alaska Geographic, ISSN 0361-1353; Key title Alaska Geographic.

THE ALASKA GEOGRAPHIC SOCIETY is a non-profit organization exploring new frontiers of knowledge across the lands of the Polar Rim, learning how other men in other countries live in their Norths, putting the geography book back in the classroom, exploring new methods of teaching and learning — sharing the excitement of discovery in man's wonderful new world north of 51°16'.

MEMBERS OF THE SOCIETY receive *ALASKA GEOGRAPHIC®*, a quality magazine that devotes each quarterly issue to monographic in-depth coverage of a northern geographic region or resource-oriented subject.

MEMBERSHIP DUES in The Alaska Geographic Society are $39 per year; $43 to non-U.S. addresses. (Eighty percent of each year's dues is for a one-year subscription to *ALASKA GEOGRAPHIC®*.) Order from The Alaska Geographic Society, Box 93370, Anchorage, AK 99509-3370; phone (907) 258-2515.

PRICE TO NONMEMBERS THIS ISSUE, $14.95 ($18.95 Canadian)

MATERIALS SOUGHT: The editors of *ALASKA GEOGRAPHIC®* seek a wide variety of informative material on the lands north of 51°16' on geographic subjects — anything to do with resources and their uses (with heavy emphasis on quality color photography) — from all the lands of the Polar Rim and the economically related North Pacific Rim. We cannot be responsible for submissions not accompanied by sufficient postage for return by certified mail. Payments are made for all material upon publication.

CHANGE OF ADDRESS: The post office does not automatically forward *ALASKA GEOGRAPHIC®* when you move. To ensure continuous service, notify us six weeks before moving. Send us your new address and zip code (and moving date), your old address and zip code, and if possible send a mailing label from a copy of *ALASKA GEOGRAPHIC®*. Send this information to *ALASKA GEOGRAPHIC®* Mailing Offices, 130 Second Avenue South, Edmonds, WA 98020-9989.

MAILING LISTS: We have begun making our members' names and addresses available to carefully screened publications and companies whose products and activities may be of interest to you. If you would prefer not to receive such mailings, please so advise us, and include your mailing label (or your name and address if label is not available).

The Library of Congress has cataloged this serial publication as follows:

Alaska Geographic. v.1-
[Anchorage, Alaska Geographic Society] 1972-
v. ill. (part col.) 23 x 31 cm.
Quarterly
Official publication of The Alaska Geographic Society.
Key title: Alaska geographic, ISSN 0361-1353.

1. Alaska — Description and travel — 1959-
— Periodicals. I. Alaska Geographic Society.

F901.A266   917.98'04'505   72-92087

Library of Congress 75[79112]   MARC-S

Postmaster: Send address changes to *ALASKA GEOGRAPHIC®*, 130 Second Ave. South Edmonds, WA 98020

ABOUT THIS ISSUE: The Alaska Geographic staff compiled this review of Katmai country. We thank Superintendent Ray Bane and his staff at Katmai National Park and Preserve, Manager Ron Hood and his staff at Becharof National Wildlife Refuge, and Betsy Yount of the U.S. Geological Survey for their assistance in answering questions and in reviewing the manuscript. For detailed information on the birds and flowers of Becharof we thank former refuge staff member Randall Wilk and his wife, Karen. We are grateful to Kim Heacox for his firsthand account of life along the Katmai coast, and to Bill Sherwonit for a close look at the McNeil River State Game Sanctuary.

As always, we appreciate the efforts of the many fine photographers whose work captures the spirit and beauty of Katmai country.

Cover: *Clouds from a summer storm create light and dark contrasts on the slopes of Baked Mountain in the Valley of Ten Thousand Smokes.* (David Rhode)

Previous page: *The McNeil River State Game Sanctuary was set aside for the large brown bears which gather here to feed each summer when the salmon return to spawn.* (David Rhode)

Contents

Ken Taylor (left) and Steve McCutcheon show off their king salmon catch at the town of King Salmon, major transportation hub for Katmai country. (Courtesy of Steve McCutcheon)

This Katmai edition of *Alaska Geographic®* speaks well for itself...a good review of how it happened...the great explosion...and what there is to see today. An eruption of the magnitude such as Katmai probably can best be seen in these reflective years long after the main event. Today it has an awesome beauty and the waters and the hills and meadows are relatively plentiful with wild things, but what is least understood is how long it has taken to get back tree growth, fish and four-legged animal life, even firm ground.

Unfortunately this Alaska Peninsula area, before modern airplane transportation, was little known and little populated. The salmon packers came and went in a short summer, and there were few scattered residents in widely separated small settlements. Biologists had much else to do in other more accessible areas, so there was little, if any, year by year assessment of how the land "came back."

But it is easy to comprehend that when Katmai blew, almost total desolation followed. Grasses were buried, animals in great numbers either fled or died, streams and lakes became choked with ash and sulfurous acids. We wonder, did the birds flee successfully, or did they flutter and die in convulsive confusion?

But the land has come back, and like the reclamation of glacier-scoured land, so has Nature continued to heal the wounds of Katmai.

We remember, traveling the Alaska Peninsula country, when the first moose came into the Nushagak country from burgeoning populations in the Kenai and Susitna areas in the late thirties. Soon there were "a dozen or so moose" occasionally sighted in the lakes area of Katmai. On down the peninsula, in the early forties, there were only an estimated 250 Grants caribou (a blockier animal than the Barren Ground species), ranging in the lower peninsula area between Port Heiden and Port Moller. Today caribou range on to Unalaska Island across False Pass at the tip of the Alaska Peninsula, and from one end of the peninsula to the other, there are large numbers of both caribou and moose where not so many years ago there were none.

That, perhaps, is the essence of the Katmai story...the wonderful recuperative strength of the natural world of which we are a part. The world changes constantly, in a zillion ways, and we are part of it.

Will there be a repetition of Katmai? Some day, or soon?

All along the elephant's trunk of the Alaska Peninsula and the Aleutians, the mountains are smoking.

Sincerely,

Robert A. Henning

Robert A. Henning
President
Alaska Geographic Society

Reddish-brown ash flow fills the lower end of the Valley of Ten Thousand Smokes. (Thomas P. Miller, USGS)

The Land

Mention Katmai country to anyone familiar with Alaska and they are likely to conjure up two images: bears and volcanoes. True, the region boasts one of the highest densities of brown bears in the world, and, although no official figures are available, the region's bruins are probably the most-photographed non-zoo bears on earth. Also true, a visit to Katmai National Park's Valley of Ten Thousand Smokes leaves one with a much greater respect for the forces of nature.

But while bears and volcanoes are definitely important, Katmai country offers much, much more. The region is bounded on the east by the rich coastal waters of Shelikof Strait and on the west by the equally rich waters of Bristol Bay. Katmai country takes in 1.2-million-acre

Ash flow from the 1912 eruption lost mobility and came to a halt along the Ukak River at the lower end of the Valley of Ten Thousand Smokes. (Thomas P. Miller, USGS)

Becharof National Wildlife Refuge, whose main feature is 458-square-mile Becharof Lake, second largest in Alaska; McNeil River State Game Sanctuary; and, of course, 4-million-acre Katmai National Park and Preserve. Adding in the communities of Egegik, King Salmon, Naknek and South Naknek completes a region that offers a diversity of topographic features.

Many peaks of the Aleutian Range, which hugs the Pacific coast, are active volcanoes and several others lie dormant, having erupted in historic times. Highest mountain in the region is 7,606-foot Mount Denison, and several other peaks also exceed 7,000 feet.

To the southeast of the range lies the coast of Shelikof Strait, a narrow strip characterized by deep bays and fiords, rocky shoreline and many islands. The waters are rich in marine life which forms the basis of a valuable commercial fishery.

On the northwest side of the Aleutian Range the land slopes, becoming flatter, poorly drained

Rugged cliffs typical of much of the Katmai coast rebuff turbulent seas from Shelikof Strait. Few visitors reach Katmai country from the coast, preferring instead to fly to King Salmon and enter from the more gentle western side. (Jim Shives)

and dominated by many streams and lakes, the largest of which are Becharof and Naknek. Three of the region's four major communities are located on the Naknek River, a 35-mile channel linking Naknek Lake and Kvichak Bay, an arm of Bristol Bay, hub of commercial fishing in southwest Alaska.

The area's climate varies dramatically, with winters alternating between extremely cold, dry weather from the north and warm, wet and windy weather from the southern Bering Sea. This southern weather is the primary influence in summer, bringing high winds, mild temperatures, clouds and frequent precipitation. On the Pacific slopes of the Aleutian Range, precipitation can exceed 200 inches; closer to the Bristol Bay coast the figure drops to 60 inches. Summer temperatures in Katmai National Park can be anywhere from 50 to 80 F, however, freezing temperatures can be encountered at higher elevations any time of year. Winter extremes range from an average low of around 20 F at Brooks Camp to as low as minus 40 F in the mountains. Violent williwaws also occur, reaching recorded velocities within the park of more than 50 miles per hour.

The National Geographic Society, sponsors of the first scientific expedition to enter Katmai after the 1912 eruption, gave its name to Geographic Harbor at the head of Amalik Bay on the Katmai coast. (Bud Rice)

Geology

In 1884, census agent Ivan Petroff included a lengthy description of Katmai country in his *Report on the Population, Industries and Resources of Alaska in the Tenth Census*, observing:

The country between Bering Sea and the Alpine chain of mountains extending along the eastern shore is a gradually ascending plain, dotted with lakes. . . . In the northern portion of the [Alaska] peninsula a belt of timber reaches down in the center to the vicinity of Lake Becharof, but beyond this the forest disappears, and only the deep ravines exhibit a stunted growth of creeping willow and alder brush.

The reindeer browse in herds all over this region, retreating during the summer up to their inaccessible retreats among the snowy peaks of the mountain range, where they are often seen by the traveler below as a moving line of black dots winding around the summits. During the autumn and winter they seek the vicinity of the lakes and scatter over the tundra, where they are hunted with comparative ease.

Foxes, land otters, martens and minks are plentiful throughout this section, and the gigantic brown bear of continental Alaska rivals the native fisherman in the wholesale destruction of the finny inhabitants of lake and stream.

When Capt. James Cook cruised Cook Inlet in 1785, he named the point on the southeast entrance to Sukoi Bay Cape Douglas in honor of his friend, Dr. John Douglas, canon of Windsor. Douglas Glacier flows down from 7,000-foot Mount Douglas, a dormant volcano. (Nina Faust)

Roger Semler stands by an active fumarole on the slopes of 3,695-foot Baked Mountain near the head of the Valley of Ten Thousand Smokes in Katmai National Park. (Bud Rice)

Yellowish-tinged sulfur coats surrounding rock near this active fumarole on 7,600-foot Mount Griggs, east of the Valley of Ten Thousand Smokes. (Bud Rice)

This cross section of a fossil fumarole along the upper River Lethe shows encrustations of minerals deposited by hot gases rising from ash flow during the 1912 eruption. These fumaroles were as hot as 1,200 F when first explored four years after the eruption; most had cooled and died out by the 1930s. (Terry Keith, USGS)

Parts of the area are unchanged today. But the tranquility of a protected bay, the silence in the pristine, snow-capped mountains, even the eerie solitude of the Valley of Ten Thousand Smokes, is deceiving: Mother Nature has not been napping in Katmai country. Today, subduction — movement of the Pacific Ocean plate northward under the North American continent — makes this one of the most seismically active areas in the world. One product of this subduction is the "Ring of Fire," a chain of volcanoes, of which the Aleutian Range is a segment, that rim the Pacific Ocean. A major earthquake or eruption may occur at any time. Other geologic forces at work in Katmai are volcanism, mountain building and erosion by ice, wind and water.

Geologists speculate that seas covered what is now the Alaska Peninsula about 150 million years ago. Fossils of marine animals are common in the sedimentary rocks around Katmai. Two episodes of volcanic activity and mountain building occurred between 90 million and 10 million years ago, pushing the peninsula up

Among the youngest in the world, this glacier has formed inside the rim of Katmai caldera. (Bud Rice)

from beneath these seas.

During the Pleistocene Epoch, which began 2 million years ago and ended 10,000 to 15,000 year ago, glaciers covering peninsula uplands gouged deep U-shaped canyons from previously unremarkable river valleys. Glacial melting caused broad outwash plains to form at the mouths of these canyons, and terminal moraines — piles of rubble pushed by moving glaciers — built up to dam streams and create many of the region's lakes, including Becharof.

More recent glacial activity is visible in Katmai National Park near Brooks Camp. Ending about 10,000 years ago, the Brooks Lake Glaciation scoured the landscape, leaving depressions now occupied by several nearby lakes. Today, there are hundreds of glaciers along the crest of the Aleutian Range, many more than 5 miles long.

One fiery volcanic episode in June 1912 forever altered the landscape in a portion of Katmai country. On the afternoon of June 6, following six days of earthquakes, a thunderous blast sounded as an immense column of smoke billowed from Novarupta Volcano. The eruption deposited about 6 cubic miles of incandescent ash and pumice in a layer at least an inch deep over an estimated area of 30,000 square miles.

The plug of Novarupta sticks out of the volcano's summit; behind is Falling Mountain, a dacite dome formed within the Holocene (the period from 10,000 to 15,000 years ago to the present). (Thomas P. Miller, USGS)

A hiker enjoys the view from the top of Novarupta. The plug atop the volcano is composed of rhyolite, a type of igneous rock similar to granite but with a finer grain. (Bud Rice)

Dan Unsworth, 12, hefts rocks en route to the Valley of Ten Thousand Smokes. Despite their size, the rocks are lightweight, made of volcanic pumice. Powdered pumice is used commercially as a polish and abrasive. (Janice Schofield)

Swim like a rock does not always mean a quick trip to the bottom: These lightweight pumice rocks are floating in Naknek Lake. Pumice is formed when gas-rich molten material cools around the gas bubbles, creating a sponge-like or frothy rock. (George Wuerthner)

Steam puffs from active fumaroles at the summit of Mount Mageik (7,250 feet). (Judy Fierstein, USGS)

Steam and gas erupt from Mount Peulik, on the southeast shore of Becharof Lake, on April 5, 1977. Translation of the peak's Aleut name means "Smoky Mountain". (Steve McCutcheon)

Chemical precipitates, commonly including gypsum, color the rocks on 3,786-foot Broken Mountain in Katmai National Park. (Charles Kay)

Trace ashfalls were recorded as far away as the Puget Sound area, 1,500 miles distant.

Ash flowing from the volcano buried the Ukak River valley up to 700 feet deep, creating a large plain where vaporized streams, rainwater and volcanic gases formed countless streams and fumaroles, vents from which hot gases escape. Remnant of the eruption is the Valley of Ten Thousand Smokes, a 30-square-mile moonscape of richly colored yellow, red and tan ash. Preservation of the valley, today a major attraction, was one of the main reasons President Woodrow Wilson set aside 1,700 square miles, including all of the eruption area, as a national monument in 1918.

Volcanism is currently a major geologic force at work in Katmai. Today, the most active volcanoes in Katmai country include Mount Trident, which erupted in 1968, and mounts Martin and Mageik, which commonly emit steam. Major eruptions in historic times include Mount Peulik (1814 and 1852), Mount Katmai (1912, 1921 and 1962), Mount Mageik (1927) and Mount Chiginigak (1929). In 1977, two maars, volcanic explosion craters, were formed in the tundra northwest of Mount Peulik. Earthquakes

Steff Lotscher hikes along a snow-filled riverbed. Ash-covered snow melts unevenly, leaving these egg-carton-like bumps.
(Chlaus Lotscher)

One of Katmai country's active volcanoes, 6,050-foot Mount Martin has nearly constant activity from fumaroles in its crater (shown in the inset photo). (Both, Thomas P. Miller, USGS)

are frequently felt in the region.

One distinctive geologic feature related to volcanism is the Katmai Caldera Glaciers, two small glaciers which formed in the caldera created after Mount Katmai's summit collapsed when Novarupta erupted in 1912.

All areas of recent volcanism are potential sources of geothermal energy. During his reconnaissance of southwestern Alaska in 1898, U.S. Geological Survey (USGS) geologist Josiah Spurr observed a large stream of hot water coming from a volcano on the east side of Katmai Pass, and extensive hot springs on the west side of the pass. Today there is a hot springs at Gas Rocks near Mount Peulik, in Becharof National Wildlife Refuge.

Mineral Resources

One of the first written references to mineral potential in Katmai country appeared in Hubert Bancroft's *History of Alaska, 1730-1885* (1886), which noted: "Petroleum of good quality has been found floating on the surface of a lake near Mount Katmai on the Alaska Peninsula." An oil seepage near Katmai Bay had been reported about 20 years earlier, and such seepages were known to occur around Becharof Lake and in the area west of Puale Bay. Between 1903 and 1904, several exploratory oil wells were drilled between Becharof Lake and Puale Bay; five more wells were completed between 1923 and 1926 near Mount Peulik; and two more were drilled

A stream has cut this 50-foot-deep chasm in the Valley of Ten Thousand Smokes. The ash flow is easily eroded, thus running water cuts through it like a knife through butter.
(Thomas P. Miller, USGS)

in 1940 and 1959 just east of Island Arm of Becharof Lake. None of these wells yielded oil or gas in commercial quantities, and all were plugged and abandoned.

There has been relatively little exploration for minerals in Katmai country. Although gold played a role in the history of the region, it was primarily gold found elsewhere: Katmai Pass was an important shortcut for goldseekers en route to Nome around the turn of the century. Some coarse gold was discovered in the area in 1907, in the upper valley of the King Salmon River. In 1925, W.R. Smith of USGS reported that the only known mineral deposit of economic value in the region was the Cape Kubugakli gold placer, located about 25 miles south of Mount Katmai on the coast of Shelikof Strait. Discovered in 1915 by Jack and Fred Mason, the claim yielded 160 ounces of gold between 1915 and 1923. Trace amounts of antimony, lead, copper and molybdenum were also found there. Around 1918 some development work, including a test shipment of ore, was done on two copper prospects, one near Kamishak Bay and the other near Kukak Bay, but actual production never occurred.

Perhaps the most successful mineral

Savonoski Crater, a hole in the sedimentary rocks located between Mount Katmai and the Savonoski River, was studied in the 1960s. The resulting theory is that it is either a meteoric crater or a volcanic vent scraped clean by glacial activity. (Betsy Yount, USGS)

Fast-growing shrubs hide the remains of a mule-drawn road grader used in oil exploration at Becharof National Wildlife Refuge about 1925. (Ron Hood, USFWS)

Remnants of 1904 oil well drilling activity from Costello #2 litter the tundra of Becharof National Wildlife Refuge. (Ron Hood, USFWS)

development in the region was made possible by the eruption of Novarupta and other area volcanoes: In 1947, six sites, including Geographic Harbor, Takli Island and Kukak Bay, were examined to determine their potential as a source of volcanic pumice for building materials. By 1952, pumice was being mined at Geographic Harbor and shipped to Anchorage for the manufacture of lightweight building blocks.

Plants and Animals

The varied environment of Katmai country supports at least three distinct types of vegetation: coastal forest, taiga and tundra. The region is the western limit for coastal forests of western hemlock and Sitka spruce, and the southern limit for taiga, mixed forests made up of poplar, alder, willow, birch and white spruce with a thick carpet of mosses and lichens on the forest floor. Two types of tundra are represented: Alpine tundra occurs above treeline (about 1,000 feet) and consists of dwarf birch and willow, alpine blueberry, crowberry and Labrador tea. Wet tundra is found in areas where permafrost prevents proper drainage, resulting in shallow ponds and swampy marshes and such plants as

A brown bear and her cub go clamming in the sand along Geographic Harbor. According to the photographer, the sow would thump the ground, looking for a good spot to dig. Once a promising location was found, she would dig in, often up to her shoulders, to retrieve the clam. (Betsy Yount, USGS)

Inky caps grow in the woods near Brooks River. As these fungi age, they decompose into a pool of black, inklike fluid.
(Janice Schofield)

cottongrass, lichens, lowbush cranberry and Labrador tea.

Little vegetation grows in the Valley of Ten Thousand Smokes, where the abrasiveness of windblown ash makes it difficult for plants to establish themselves. In some places, an almost microscopic black moss clings to the surface, and there are areas in the valley which support grasses, sedges, willows and even a few hardy wildflowers.

The elegant, violet wild geranium grows in suitable habitat throughout Katmai country. (Janice Schofield)

Although they prefer salmon, omniverous brown bears will eat whatever is available. (David Rhode)

Such rich diversity provides habitat for a large number of mammals, fish and birds.

Undisputed king of Katmai country is the brown bear. Each summer, visitors from throughout the world come to watch and photograph these massive animals, which can reach 8 or 9 feet tall and weigh up to 1,500 pounds, as they gather to feed at salmon-spawning streams. The region not only supports one of the greatest densities of brown bears anywhere, Katmai National Park shelters the largest unhunted population of coastal brown bears in the world.

Because protection of bears and their access to their habitat is a primary consideration at Katmai, McNeil River and Becharof refuge, almost every activity in the area is governed by its impact on the bears and the safety of bear-human interaction.

Although the bears of Katmai country are best known for their appetite for fish, they actually eat a wide range of plants and animals, depending on the area and season. Along the coast, bears swim to nearshore islands to feed on seabird eggs and scavenge marine mammal carcasses that have washed ashore. At other times, the animals feed on sedges and marsh plants or crowberries, which are abundant in alpine fields. After a summer of voracious eating, the bears hibernate in dens from November until April. Within their dens in mid-winter, sows may give birth to one or two cubs, which usually stay with their mother through one or

Caribou roam Katmai country on the west side of the Aleutian Range. The Alaska Peninsula herd migrates through the lowlands, but animals can be found high on a snowfield or along the beach trying to escape annoying insects.
(Karen Jettmar)

two summers. Occasionally, sows will adopt orphaned cubs.

Caribou of the northern Alaska Peninsula herd range throughout Katmai country. Some forage within Becharof refuge, and each year in late summer thousands of the animals can be seen near Whale Mountain, along the north side of Becharof Lake. In late winter, the caribou

begin their migration to calving grounds farther south on the peninsula.

Moose are also important residents of Katmai country, feeding on dwarf birch and willow and calving in the dense forests. Other land mammals to be found in the area include beavers, ermine, river otters, lynx, porcupines, red foxes, snowshoe hares and wolves.

Several species of marine mammals inhabit the coastal waters of Shelikof Strait. Sea otters feed offshore, enjoying a large population today after being hunted nearly to extinction less than a century ago. Harbor seals and sea lions, as many as 5,000 at a time in Puale Bay, haul out on beaches. Beluga whales can sometimes be seen in bays or inlets, and other whale species may use nearshore waters.

The diverse environment of Katmai country provides abundant habitat for about 150 species of visiting or nesting seabirds, waterfowl, birds of prey and shorebirds. During migration, thousands of waterfowl such as northern pintails, greater scaups, American wigeons, mallards, green-winged teals, tundra swans, northern shovelers, common goldeneyes, oldsquaws, gadwalls, harlequin ducks, white-winged, surf and black scoters and common and red-breasted

While not as numerous as caribou in Becharof National Wildlife Refuge, moose do inhabit forested areas, particularly those adjacent to Katmai National Park. Moose are found in appropriate habitat throughout the park and usually can be seen in summer feeding in ponds from the road leading to the Valley of Ten Thousand Smokes. (Jim Shives)

A beaver stashes a sapling into the complex of twigs and mud that forms its house in a small pond near downtown King Salmon. (Jim Simmen)

Gulls and Steller sea lions have taken over Shakun Rock northeast of Hallo Bay on Katmai's coast. (Nina Faust)

Mergansers wait on the shore of Brooks River. These waterfowl usually breed where ponds, lakes and rivers provide plenty of fresh water in which to feed. (David Rhode)

The penetrating eyes of a great horned owl search for prey from this perch near Brooks Lake. (Bud Rice)

mergansers use ponds, rivers and streams in the area; many also breed there.

Studies conducted in Becharof refuge from 1985 to 1987 identified a number of shorebirds, including least sandpiper, semipalmated plover, dunlin, short-billed dowitcher, red-necked phalarope and greater yellowlegs, as common nesters within the refuge. Frequent occupants of lowland wet tundra include mew gulls, Arctic terns and long-tailed and parasitic jaegers.

Katmai country's rugged Pacific coastline provides nesting habitat for a variety of seabirds. Two seabird colonies in Puale Bay are among the largest on the Alaska Peninsula coastline.

Species to be found include common and thick-billed murres, whose colonies can contain as many as 80,000 birds, black-legged kittiwakes, glaucous-winged gulls and lesser numbers of tufted puffins and cormorants.

Bald eagles are the most visible bird of prey in the region, commonly nesting along the coast and congregating along salmon-spawning streams in summer and fall. Other birds of prey seen in the area include several species of owls, northern harriers, rough-legged hawks, Peale's peregrine falcons and gyrfalcons.

These raucous glaucous-winged gulls are members of the clean-up crew for Katmai country. While capable of hunting prey and harassing the young of other bird species, the gulls readily scavenge assorted human garbage or scraps of fish left behind by bears. (Kim Heacox)

A bald eagle comes in for a landing on a ridge overlooking Mikfik Creek. The creek flows into McNeil Cove just south of McNeil River. (Bill Sherwonit)

The waters in and around Katmai country provide habitat for five species of salmon, rainbow and lake trout, Dolly Varden, arctic char, arctic grayling, pike and burbot, which can be found in hundreds of area lakes, streams and rivers.

In terms of its ultimate commercial value, the most important fish in the region is salmon. Each June, adult fish arrive from the sea to begin the journey to their spawning streams. Some soon become food for brown bears and other predators (including man); others continue upstream through late summer or early fall, when they spawn and then die in gravel-bottomed streams and lakes, such as Brooks River or Island Arm of Becharof Lake. Even after they die, the fish continue to provide food for a number of wildlife species, and their decomposing bodies provide nutrients to sustain the young fish that hatch the following spring. Thus, salmon are not only crucial to the economy, they represent a vital link in the region's food chain.

The most important sport fish in Katmai country are undoubtedly rainbow trout, which reach trophy-size in area waters. These rainbows are sought after in great numbers, but since it takes three to six years for them to reach reproductive maturity, the Park Service encourages releasing any rainbow trout caught within Katmai National Park and Preserve.

Commercial Fishing

The rich waters of Shelikof Strait southeast of Katmai country support a number of economically important commercial fisheries. Fishermen from the Kodiak area take salmon, herring, several types of groundfish and a variety of shellfish from the beaches, bays and offshore waters.

Katmai area salmon runs are an integral part of the Kodiak salmon fishery. According to the Alaska Department of Fish and Game, streams buried in the 1912 eruption have completely recovered to become major salmon-spawning sites. The 1988 catch included 1.75 million pink salmon, 392,000 chums, 55,000 cohos and 15,000 sockeye salmon. No king salmon were reported.

In 1988, 174 tons of herring were taken in Shelikof Strait, bound for the Japanese sac-roe market. A pollock roe fishery was started in the area in the early 1980s; the roe is sold on the Asian market.

Some crab are also taken in Katmai waters, 100,000 pounds of Dungeness and 400,000 pounds of tanner in 1987. The tanner catch is down from its peak years, when a harvest of 2 to 3 million pounds was not uncommon, but remains lucrative because the smaller catch has driven prices up. The king crab fishery in Shelikof Strait was closed in 1983, but king crab are becoming more abundant there and the fishery may reopen in the future.

Before 1975, Swikshak Bay, 25 miles south of Cape Douglas, was the site of a commercial razor clam fishery. In 1974, the last year of the fishery, 200,000 pounds of clams for canning were taken, down from 420,000 pounds harvested in the peak year of 1960. The 1964 Good Friday earthquake caused changes in the beach which made the clams less accessible, and

Left - *A fisherman in the Bay of Islands area of Naknek Lake shows off his catch of northern pike.* (David Rhode)

Below - *This rainbow trout in spawning colors was taken from the Naknek River near King Salmon.* (USFWS)

Commercial fishermen prepare to take red salmon from Mikfik Creek in McNeil River State Game Sanctuary.
(Bill Sherwonit)

The Alaska Department of Fish and Game maintains this salmon resource station on Becharof Lake.
(David Rhode)

the fishery declined. There is no commercial clam harvest today, but the area is still popular with sport clam diggers who fly over from Naknek and King Salmon, and some Dungeness crab fishermen dig the clams for bait.

A small, irregular shrimp fishery exists in the area; the 1987 catch was 10,000 pounds, but no shrimp were taken in 1988. A scallop fishery began in the mid-1980s, with a dredge bringing up about 100,000 pounds of the shellfish each year from an offshore area south of Cape Douglas.

The major commercial groundfishery in Shelikof is pollock, although the catch has been depressed in recent years. Preliminary figures show the 1988 catch in Shelikof Strait was about 33 million pounds. Small numbers of flounder and cod are also taken in the strait, as is halibut, although no catch figures were available.

Editor's note: *To the west of Katmai country stretches Bristol Bay, home of one of the world's richest salmon runs. Value of the commercial salmon catch varies from year to year, but from 1980 to 1987 it ranged between $81 million and $144 million. Although this fishery is crucial to the economies of Egegik, Naknek, South Naknek and King Salmon, Bristol Bay is not within the boundaries of Katmai country, and therefore its fishery will not be covered in this book. For more information on the Bristol Bay fishery, see* Alaska's Salmon Fisheries, Alaska Geographic® *Vol. 10, No. 3* (see page 94).

While waiting for an opening, a portion of the Bristol Bay red salmon fleet ties up at Naknek. These boats fish the largest red salmon run in the world. (Jim Simmen)

The Day the Earth Roared

Editor's note: This material is excerpted from the Katmai section of Alaska's Volcanoes: Northern Link in the Ring of Fire, *Vol. 4, No. 1, of Alaska Geographic. We thank Betsy Yount of the U.S. Geological Survey and Dr. Juergen Kienle and Dr. David Stone of the University of Alaska for their help with this text.*

In early June 1912 the three-peaked spire known as Mount Katmai, after apparently centuries of quiescence, burst in an eruption that was the greatest volcanic catastrophe in the recorded history of Alaska.

More than 6 cubic miles of ash and pumice, estimated to have a total weight of 33 billion tons, were blown into the air from the mountain and adjacent vents in an area now known as the Valley of Ten Thousand Smokes. Later measurements of thickness of ash led to a conclusion that almost all of the material erupted from smaller vents in the valley and a new volcano, Novarupta, and that Mount Katmai played a subordinate role in a series of eruptions.

Modern researchers have suggested that the relationship between Mount Katmai and Novarupta was that of a storage vessel and relief valve. Novarupta's base is located thousands of feet in elevation below Katmai, and some authorities now believe that a fissure system, newly formed at the time, stretched across the intervening six miles and connected the two volcanoes underground. This fissure system drained Katmai's reservoir to the point where the mountain could not support its own weight and it collapsed, creating a caldera 1.6 miles deep and more than 3.2 miles in diameter.

For more than a quarter of a century, the most complete account of the eruption was that prepared by Dr. Robert F. Griggs, an Ohio State University botanist, who led four expeditions into the area in the years immediately following the eruption. His efforts to reconstruct events preceding the eruption itself were often seemingly in conflict.

Dr. Griggs missed the significance of Novarupta in the explosive chain of events. But his detailed investigation determined that as much as five days before the eruption, earthquakes began to be felt at Katmai village, 20 miles from the volcano. Villagers were frightened and on June 4 moved to a camp 10 miles down the coast. When the eruption broke out on June 5, they proceeded another 20 miles along the coast to Puale Bay. About the same time, villagers at Savonoski, northwest of Mount Katmai, made their way to Naknek, 50 miles away.

On the evening of June 5, an eruptive cloud was seen from Puale Bay and during the morning of June 6 several large explosions were

heard. At about 1 p.m. the same day, the great explosions of the main phase of the eruption began and continued for more than two days.

Fragmentary accounts from the area at the time suggest that fairly strong eruptions continued for several weeks, after which the amount of ash being erupted diminished, although tremors and gas-laden explosions continued.

No seismographs recorded the preliminary earthquakes but quakes accompanying the first few days of the eruption itself, however, were picked up by recording devices in Victoria, British Columbia, and in Seattle. Air shock waves of the explosions were reported to have been seen from Seldovia, 150 miles away, and the noises to have been heard at Juneau, 750 miles from the site.

After long study, Dr. Griggs summarized his understanding of the eruption:

In 1916 Dr. Robert Griggs visited Katmai, discovering and naming the Valley of Ten Thousand Smokes. In 1922 in his book, The Valley of Ten Thousand Smokes, *he commented on the find: "No photograph can convey more than a slight conception of the wonder and majesty of this sight as it first burst on our vision on crossing the Pass."* (Robert F. Griggs, © National Geographic Society)

"Just before Mount Katmai exploded, the valley, through which ran the old trail across the peninsula, burst open in many places, and a

Members of Robert Griggs' 1919 expedition to Katmai fry bacon over a steaming fumarole. The hot steam emerged so forcefully that the pan had to be held down to balance the pressure. (E. C. Kolb, © National Geographic Society)

great mass of incandescent material poured through the fissures. This molten magma was surcharged with gases . . . . Flowing down the valley under gravity, it filled an area more than 50 square miles in extent with a deposit of fine ground tuff.

"After the extension of solid material, the valley continued to emit gases in great volume, forming millions of fumaroles, which constitute one of the most awe-inspiring spectacles. This feature ... was discovered by the expedition . . . in 1916 . . . and named 'The Valley of Ten Thousand Smokes.'"

Much of Dr. Griggs' information came from the logs of two ships cruising in Alaska waters at the time of the eruptions.

On June 6 the steamer *Dora* was moving through Shelikof Strait bound for Kodiak and Capt. C.B. McMullen noted in the ship's log:

"Left Uyak at 8:15 a.m., a strong westerly breeze and fine clear weather. At 1 o'clock p.m., while entering Kupreanot Straits [Kupreanof Strait], sighted a heavy cloud of smoke directly astern, raising from the Alaska Peninsula. I took a bearing of same, which I made out to be Katmai Volcano, distance about 55 miles away. The smoke arose and spread in the sky following the vessel, and by 3:00 p.m. was directly over us, having traveled at the rate of 20 miles an hour. . . .

"At 6:30 p.m. when off Spruce Rock, which is about 3 1/2 miles from Mill Bay Rocks and the entrance to Kodiak, ashes commenced to fall and in a few minutes we were in complete darkness, not even the water over the ship's side could be seen. . . .

"Heavy thunder and lightning commenced early in the afternoon and continued throughout the night. Birds of all species kept falling on the deck in a helpless condition. The temperature rose owing to the heat of the volcanic ash, the latter penetrating into all parts of the ship, even down into the engine room."

Capt. K.W. Perry, in the June 7 log entry of the U.S. Revenue Cutter *Manning*, at Kodiak reported:

"All streams and wells have now become choked, about five inches of ash having fallen, and water was furnished inhabitants by the Manning and by a schooner.

"At noon ashes began to fall again, increased until 1:00 p.m., visibility was 50 feet. Abject terror took possession of the place. At 2:00 p.m. pitch darkness shut in."

As indicated by the logs, ash fall of the eruption was mainly in the quadrant east-southeastward across Kodiak Island, with a minor lobe to the north.

According to Griggs' detailed studies, an area of 3,000 square miles was covered by ash a foot or more deep, and 30,000 square miles by more than an inch of ash. Small ash falls were also recorded in Fairbanks, 500 miles away, Juneau, 750 miles distant, and in the Puget Sound region, about 1,500 miles away.

Appreciable amounts of extremely fine ash blown into the stratosphere remained in suspension for months and caused spectacular red sunsets in many parts of the globe. The ash-laden atmosphere, because of its ability to reflect radiant heat from the sun, also reportedly reduced average world temperatures 2 degrees Fahrenheit during the following year. And some scientists have theorized that the highly unlikely event of a series of eruptions like that at Katmai could bring on a new ice age.

History

In Ancient Times

After the Pleistocene glaciers retreated from the Alaska Peninsula, two separate cultures developed in Katmai country, one on each side of the Aleutian Range. People to the west lived in the lowlands and lake region, subsisting on salmon and other fish; those along the eastern coast depended on the abundant marine mammals.

Oldest evidence of human occupation in the area is near the Bristol Bay coast, where a group of hunters lived about 8,000 years ago. Within Katmai National Park, earliest occupation dates from about 4,500 years ago, when groups of people lived along the shores of Brooks and Naknek lakes.

At 3,315 feet, Mount LaGorce overlooks Munson Cove on the north shore of Iliuk Arm of Naknek Lake. (Bud Rice)

Archaeologists have identified four distinct periods of prehistoric occupation on the west side of the mountains, beginning with the Kittewick Period, during which two groups of inland hunter-gatherers eked out a living from the forests and the tundra until about 1900 B.C. At that time, known as the Gomer Period, the first inhabitants related to Eskimos appeared, subsisting more by salmon fishing than by hunting. This culture, which continued for 800 years, was noted for the craftsmanship of its chipped stone implements.

Following a 700-year gap, a group of hunters and fishermen occupied the area during the Brooks River Period, about 400 B.C., introducing new cultural traits such as the use of pottery. The final period, the Naknek Period, began about 1,000 years ago. Gravel-tempered pottery and ground stone tools (particularly slate) suggest that technological changes taking place far to

The area surrounding the confluence of Ukak and Savonoski rivers has been the site of native settlements in historic and possibly prehistoric times. All settlements in this area were abandoned after the 1912 eruption of Novarupta Volcano. (George Wuerthner)

the north influenced these people.

On the other side of the mountains, occupation sites were not concentrated, but rather were spread out along the coastline. Four periods of occupation have also been identified for this area, starting with the Pacific Period from 4000 to 2000 B.C. This period represents the earliest inhabitants, who subsisted on marine mammals. The Takli Period, beginning about 2500 B.C. and persisting for 1,700 years, is characterized by the addition of several cultural traits, including use of ground slate tools.

Pottery first appeared on the coast during the Kukak Period, 1000 B.C. to A.D. 200, when people moved from small campsites to true villages. It is thought that the first contact with Natives on the other side of the Aleutian Range occurred during this period. During the Katmai Period, from A.D. 200 until the arrival of white men, communication between native groups on either side of the mountains increased gradually until the two cultures merged.

The White Man Arrives

A Russian expedition led by Vitus Bering was first to sight the Alaska Peninsula in 1741. When explorers first came to Katmai country in the late 1700s, they found peninsula Eskimos (Koniag) along the coast of Shelikof Strait and in the interior, and Aglegmiut from the Kuskokwim region living primarily on the Bristol Bay coast. Annual salmon runs and caribou migrations were the mainstays of both groups; the Koniag along the coast also depended on marine mammals.

In the mid-1800s, the aggressive Aglegmiut pushed the Koniag east from the Kvichak and

Bud Loftsteadt and Dave Snow explore the remains of a Bristol Bay double-ender left rotting high and dry near Becharof Lake.
(Ron Hood, USFWS)

and establishing themselves on the Shelikof coast.

The Russian American Company increased its foothold on the Alaska Peninsula when it opened a major trading post at Katmai village, operating it from 1799 until 1867. Inland people reached the post, located on the coast about 15 miles south of Mount Katmai, by way of Katmai Pass. Another post, Fort Suvaroff, built at the mouth of the Naknek River in the early 1800s, took advantage of the Aglegmiut's growing dependence on trade goods. From these posts, Russian Orthodox missionaries visited native villages around Katmai country, an influence evident throughout the native population today.

After the United States purchased Alaska in 1867, the Alaska Commercial Company bought most of the Russian American Company's holdings in the region. But by then competition in the fur trade had driven up the price of sea otter pelts, and the resulting slaughter nearly brought about the extinction of the species. As sea otter numbers declined, some native hunters returned to a subsistence lifestyle, others turned to a burgeoning new industry, commercial fishing.

Naknek rivers. Despite this animosity, the groups traded with each other, traveling back and forth via rugged Katmai Pass, a route through the Aleutian Range which had been used since ancient times.

By 1791, Russian American Company fur traders, exploiting the region's abundant sea otters, had moved up from the Aleutian Islands, opening a trading post on Kodiak Island (1784)

The economy around Katmai country changed forever when the Arctic Packing Company opened the area's first salmon cannery in 1884 along the Nushagak River. The company expanded in 1890, building a saltery at South Naknek. In 1893 the saltery was sold to Alaska Packers Association, which opened a cannery there the following year. Other commercial fish processors in the area included L.A. Pederson's small saltery on the north shore of the Naknek River, opened in 1890. Pederson incorporated as Naknek Packing Company and built a cannery in 1894. Bumble Bee Seafoods operated a cannery at South Naknek in the 1920s.

In the early days of commercial fishing in Bristol Bay, packers believed Dolly Varden and other species thought to prey on young salmon were threatening their valuable sockeye runs. In response, around 1920 the U.S. Bureau of Fisheries organized a program of predator control, offering bounties of up to 5 cents for each tail brought in from one of the targeted "predator" species. The program's purpose was not only to increase salmon runs, but also to provide an additional source of income for fishermen during the Depression. Funded first by the packers themselves and later by the Alaska Territorial Legislature, more than 13,000 sport fish were killed under the program just between 1920 and 1925; the program continued until 1941.

In the late 1800s, a few prospectors came to Katmai country in search of gold, coal and oil, but most left disappointed. So many goldseekers en route to Nome around the turn of the century used the trail across Katmai Pass as a shortcut, however, that the trader at Katmai village built a bunkhouse to accommodate the stampeders.

In 1898, USGS geologist Josiah Spurr made a reconnaissance of southwestern Alaska which ended with a trek across Katmai country. Spurr's account of the journey provides one of the best recorded descriptions of the region, including the Valley of Ten Thousand Smokes, before the 1912 eruption. Another description appeared in *Frank Leslie's Illustrated Newspaper* in 1891, when a reporter told of his group's campsite in a "thin little group of trees" at the 3,000-foot level of the valley.

Into the 20th Century

The June 1912 eruption of Novarupta Volcano resulted in a flurry of scientific expeditions to the area. The first was jointly initiated by USGS and the National Geographic Society, who sent George Martin to the site. Martin arrived in Kodiak in July 1912, interviewing people there and traveling along the Katmai coast looking for eyewitnesses. His report credited Mount Katmai as the source of the eruption, a theory other scientists subsequently adopted.

Dr. Robert F. Griggs, sponsored by the National Geographic Society, conducted the best known study of the eruption. In 1913 Griggs had

National Park Service workers renovate a cabin once occupied by trapper Roy Fure, a longtime resident along the shore of the Bay of Islands arm of Naknek Lake. The restored cabin is to be used as a historic site. The inset photo shows the cabin in 1980, before renovation began.
(Jim Simmen; inset, George Wuerthner)

been on Kodiak Island, examining the effects of the eruption on plant regeneration. He returned to the area several times, in 1916 entering and naming the Valley of Ten Thousand Smokes. He later described discovering the valley:

The sight that flashed into view as we surmounted the hillock was one of the most amazing visions ever beheld by mortal eye. The whole valley as far as the eye could reach was full of hundreds, no thousands — literally, tens of thousands — of smokes curling up from its fissured floor. . . . For a few moments we stood gaping at the awe-inspiring vision before us, then plunged down to get a nearer view.

It was as though all the steam engines in the world, assembled together, had popped their safety valves at once and were letting off surplus steam in concert.

Griggs' accounts of his expeditions to Katmai increased public awareness and emphasized the scientific importance of preserving the area. For this purpose, the National Geographic Society recommended that Katmai be set aside as a national park.

In 1918, President Woodrow Wilson created Katmai National Monument, a 1,700-square-mile refuge that included the entire eruption area. Subsequent additions enlarged the monument and added offshore islands to its acreage. Passage of the Alaska National Interest

These photos show a few of the adventuresome tourists who made the trip to Katmai National Monument in the 1950s. Above, a visitor at Brooks River Camp examines souvenirs in the "gift shop;" below, guests enjoy a hearty breakfast. (Both, Ward Wells Collection, Anchorage Museum)

Photographers' tents line the shore near McNeil River in summer 1953. Fourteen years later, the Alaska Legislature, at the urging of outdoorsmen, conservationists, photographers and others, established the state game sanctuary.
(Steve McCutcheon)

contains no roadhouses or trading posts, and is inaccessible to the average traveler." Between 1918 and the end of World War II, the monument was seldom visited. Military personnel returning from King Salmon after the war, however, spread word of the outstanding sport fishing, scenery and wildlife they had enjoyed at military recreation camps at the outlet of Naknek Lake and at the foot of Naknek River Rapids.

In 1953, in response to a movement to open the monument for commercial fishing, hunting, trapping and mining, the National Park Service conducted a study which concluded that the area should remain a national monument, but that there was a need for better access and more visitor facilities.

One of the champions of tourism in Katmai was Ray Petersen, who in 1950 set up a tent camp in the national monument as a tour destination for his fledgling Northern Consolidated Airline. Petersen and his partner, John Walatka, opened Angler's Paradise sport fishing camps on Lake Grosvenor and near Brooks River. Today Katmailand Inc., a company formed by Petersen and his son, operates several lodges in the park.

President Jimmy Carter set aside adjacent 1.2-million-acre Becharof National Wildlife Monument in 1978 to preserve "one of the densest known populations of the great Alaska brown bear." ANILCA made the monument part of the National Wildlife Refuge system, managed by the U.S. Fish and Wildlife Service.

Lands Conservation Act (ANILCA) in December 1980 added more than 1 million additional acres to the existing monument, and gave the entire area national park status.

Tourism was slow coming to Katmai country. In *A Guide to Alaska* (1939), author Merle Colby described Katmai as "rarely visited by steamers,

A Summer on the Katmai Coast

By Kim Heacox

Editor's note: A former ranger at Katmai, Glacier Bay and Denali national parks, Kim now writes full-time from his Anchorage home. His wife, Melanie, works for the National Park Service in Anchorage.

They should have hired a carpenter, but they got us instead — Melanie and me — two rangers sent to patrol the wild waters of the Katmai coast. There among the alder and cow parsnips of Amalik Bay we found the rotting cabin that would be our summer home.

We opened the door and water poured out. The roof sagged, one wall was partially collapsed, the stove had rusted away and every window was broken. Melanie's eyes glazed over, "Oh no, what have we done?"

Most rangers in Katmai work in Brooks Camp, the nerve center of the park where planes, people, fish and bears manage to squeeze into the same place at the same time. On a sunny afternoon in July, Brooks Camp looks and sounds like a wilderness version of La Guardia Airport. But far to the east over the rugged Aleutian Mountains lies another Katmai—the one you don't hear much about. The one few people visit. The Katmai coast.

Melanie and I had been sent here in summer 1985 to accomplish two things: rebuild the Amalik Bay cabin into a workable ranger station and patrol the 120-mile coast in a 15-foot Zodiac to monitor wildlife and commercial fishermen.

Easier said than done. Between the Katmai coast and Kodiak Island

Two major seabird colonies cling to the rugged shores of Katmai's coast. Murres and kittiwakes dominate in the colonies but a few horned puffins (shown here) and tufted puffins also make their home there.
(Kim Heacox)

A turbulent, fiery sunset over Geographic Harbor fits well in a world where volcanism and erosion continue to shape a young land. (Kim Heacox)

30 miles farther east lies Shelikof Strait, some of the roughest water in Alaska. A Zodiac in Shelikof Strait? You might have better odds in a dinghy off Cape Horn. "Don't go out in the big waves," the chief ranger had told us as we loaded two months of supplies into the Grumman Goose in King Salmon. Okay, but from everything we had heard or read, Shelikof had nothing but big waves.

So there we stood on the threshold of a cold, dreary cabin beneath a cold, dreary sky. And it started to rain. The pilot was eager to leave. We unloaded our supplies: Zodiac, outboard engine, shotgun, survival suits, freeze-dried food, a new wood-burning stove, plywood, lumber, metal siding, portable generator, electric drill, VHF and single sideband radios, duffels of wool clothing, raingear, a saw, two hammers and 2,000 nails. In a week we'd have four black thumbs, shutters on the windows and a new roof. The pilot waved goodbye and was gone. A golden-crowned sparrow sang. Then came the grand silence and a great sense of adventure. The summer was ours.

Week by week the cabin became more livable. Our carpentry skills improved and our thumbs healed. We threw out the old stove and put in the new. We rebuilt one battered wall, shored up a sagging corner and fashioned a drainage system for runoff water. New shelves held our food, books and cassettes. It wasn't just an old cabin any more, it was home. We danced to the Beatles and baked cookies inside while the wind and rain raged outside.

Later that year people from Kodiak would say 1985 was the nastiest summer they could remember in Shelikof Strait. For 23 days in July the radio crackled, "Gale warning for Shelikof Strait, seas to 15 feet." Or 20 feet, or 30. We patrolled within the protected waters of Amalik Bay and Geographic Harbor, enjoying wild scenery as we counted seabirds, harbor seals, Steller sea lions and bears.

Ah yes, bears.

One morning the entire cabin started shaking and Melanie popped out of bed, "It's an

Melanie Heacox enjoys a quiet evening reading in the Amalik Bay cabin she and Kim fixed up during their summer on the Katmai coast. (Kim Heacox)

earthquake." Then I heard a deep, low groan.

"That's not an earthquake." I grabbed the shotgun, opened the door and saw a 700-pound brown bear scratching his back on the corner of our cabin. He bolted into the brush and disappeared.

By July bears were a daily occurrence in our lives. Most would walk down the beach with little concern about the cabin and its contents. Some dug for clams at low tide. One found a large, red buoy and tried to bite it. Finally he swiped at it with his paw and jumped with fright when it popped. Two young siblings got into a wrestling match and knocked out our single sideband antenna.

But most memorable was the curious bear that suddenly rounded a corner of the cabin and walked up the porch straight at us. Imagine turning around to see a furry, pig-eyed face right out the window, staring at you. Several times I was tempted to pepper the intruding

The waters off Katmai's coast are rich in marine life, such as the Dungeness crab shown here, and have drawn fishermen to the area for decades. Park Service rangers patrol the coast, talking with fishermen who know the area best. (Kim Heacox)

bears with the shotgun, but I didn't. The real intruders, after all, were in the mirror, not out the window.

Melanie and I were not the first part-time residents in Amalik Bay. Two rangers had preceded us the year before, and Alaska Department of Fish and Game fish biologists had occupied the cabin nearly every spring since building it in 1962. The most famous resident of Amalik Bay, however, was not a human, but a horse.

In September 1956 a barge carrying 16 horses departed for Kodiak from Puale Bay where the horses had been leased for oil exploration work near Becharof Lake. Suddenly the weather worsened and high seas began flooding the barge. The skipper off-loaded the horses at Amalik and hastened on to Kodiak. What happened next remains unknown, but three stories persist: Either the owners returned for the horses and found all but one, they returned and shot all the horses but one, or they never returned and all the horses died but one. *[**Editor's note:** Carl Jones of Homer wrangled for the*

late Jack Deitz, owner of the horses, the year before the animals were taken to Becharof. He reports that no one went back for the horses. Some of the animals were injured in the off-loading, and some did not make it through the winter.]

The survivor was a bay gelding usually seen on the peninsula at the entrance to Amalik Bay. "As chance would have it, the horse's peninsula provided him with what he needed," wrote Dave Bohn in *Rambles Through an Alaskan Wild* (1979). "Ample grass near the beaches, salt, fresh water streamlets in summer, and the sand patches which he frequented. Bears and wolves must have treated him as a moose; that is, they sized him up and knew he was healthy and could kick . . . them. So they left him alone, and the years passed. The occasional visiting fishermen often saw him and one or two of them would periodically leave him carrots or lettuce, but could never persuade him to feed from the hand. As a rule, no one got closer than one hundred and fifty feet. Subsequently, as fascination with

Brown bears rule Katmai country and human residents of the area have to take precautions to avoid encounters with the powerful animals. Here Melanie Heacox lifts a board with outward-pointing nails up onto the cabin's porch. The board will be attached to the door to keep any curious bears from breaking through. (Kim Heacox)

the tale grew, low-flying pilots would check the peninsula to see if he was alive and well, and on return to King Salmon or Kodiak the question was inevitable: 'Did you see the horse?'

"Katmai's wild horse . . . had become a living legend."

In August 1973 Bohn flew out to Amalik Bay and saw the gelding. He was just in time, for in May 1974 a fisherman visiting the bay found the horse's bones, surrounded by wolf tracks. People in Kodiak estimated the horse was seven when put ashore. If so, he lived 25 years, 18 of them as a legend in Amalik Bay.

When the bad weather broke, Melanie and I hit the open water. We motored up to Kukak Bay and found 15 seiners waiting for a chum salmon opening. Pulling up to one after another, the fishermen would step out on deck and say, "Howdy, where's your boat?"

"This is our boat."

"That's your boat!" they'd say. "You must be crazy. C'mon aboard and have something to eat."

So we passed the nights talking to the most knowledgeable people on the Katmai coast, fishermen from Kodiak, Chignik, Seldovia and elsewhere who'd fished these waters for decades. Closing my eyes, I can still see them, the cigarette smoke curling around their untrimmed beards, the grease on their fingers, the laughter in their eyes. They fed us crab and baked potatoes and told us about large stern trawlers that fish winters in Shelikof Strait for pollock, rock fish and black cod. They spoke about seeing 18 bears at once in the back of Kukak Inlet, and about "more puffins that you can imagine" in Hallo Bay. They spoke about 24-hour salmon openings when the silvers were so thick they'd fill their boats in hours, when 25 seiners and 100 fishermen would flood into Swikshak Bay, when 20-year-old crewmen would earn $1,000 on good days and nothing on bad days. "It's a gambler's life," one of them told us. "If I were me I wouldn't do it."

Such was our summer on the quiet side of Katmai. We thought it would be easy to leave when the plane came to pick us up in September. But it wasn't.

Recreation

Becharof National Wildlife Refuge

Most visitors to the refuge come to hunt caribou, brown bear and moose, but Becharof also offers plentiful fishing and hiking opportunities. Mount Peulik, 4,835 feet, is easily hiked in late summer. On the mountain's southeast flank, hikers can circumnavigate Ugashik Caldera which has three big cinder cones, steaming vents and hot springs. Just to the northwest of Mount Peulik, on the shore of Becharof Lake, lie the Gas Rocks, an old volcanic plug from which carbon dioxide leaks. The escaping gas gives the water in this part of the lake the appearance of boiling. Adjacent to Gas

An active volcano, 4,835-foot Mount Peulik towers over Becharof Lake. These two landscape features symbolize the wilderness of Becharof National Wildlife Refuge, on the Alaska Peninsula south of Katmai National Park. (David Rhode)

Rocks are Ukinrek Maars, volcanic explosion craters formed in 1977.

An explosion of another kind occurs each summer when a profusion of wild flowers erupts. In the upland, where hiking is easy once travelers get above the brush line, bloom Arctic forget-me-nots, bluebells, moss campion, dryas, avens, alpine azaleas and cuckoo flowers.

In damper areas, look for lady's slipper, bog orchid, Jacob's ladder, bog saxifrage and the brilliant white tufts of cottongrass. In wet areas on the Pacific coast side you can't miss the showy Kamchatka rhododendron.

If you'd rather take a float trip than hike, try the 25- to 30-mile float down the Kejulik River to the mouth of Becharof Lake. The river heads in the Kejulik Mountains in Katmai National Park and flows through designated wilderness portions of the refuge.

Fishing is good in Becharof, just as it is in

The elegant Kamchatka rhododendron grows in bright clusters along the Pacific coast of Katmai country. (Jim Shives)

Dry, upland areas of Katmai country produce the tiny pink jewels of alpine azalea. (Jim Shives)

Birders should scan the Ugashik drainage each fall for flocks of migrating cackling Canada geese, one of the species whose nesting numbers on the Yukon-Kuskokwim delta have declined drastically in recent years. White-fronted geese stage in Island Arm of Becharof Lake, while tundra swans can be found nesting in the Kejulik valley and on north and west portions of the refuge. Small groups of double-crested cormorants and glaucous-winged gulls nest on rocky outcrops in southern Becharof Lake.

Puale Bay on the Pacific coast has two colonies of seabirds, and waterfowl nest in suitable habitat throughout the refuge. On wet tundra watch for nesting least sandpipers, dunlin and common snipe, Lapland longspurs and Savannah sparrows. At higher elevations with patches of willows look for golden-crowned and white-crowned sparrows and Wilson's, yellow and orange-crowned warblers. For birdwatchers interested in raptors, watch for bald eagles and the Peale's race of peregrine falcons along the Pacific coast, and gyrfalcons, northern harriers and short-eared owls farther inland. Rough-legged hawks also nest on rocky bluffs in inland areas.

Hiking, birdwatching and fishing are great in Becharof, but most visitors come to hunt big game, brown bear, moose and caribou in particular. The big brownies are especially noticeable around Becharof Lake, and every July and August, when red salmon are spawning, nearly every stream has a brown bear fishing on its banks.

most of Katmai country. Try Featherly Creek at the southeast end of Becharof Lake for grayling, or Gertrude Creek for king, silver, red and chum salmon, rainbow trout, arctic char and grayling. The Ruth River also has several grayling holes. The Pacific side has several unnamed streams with silver, chum and pink salmon, and just about any stream in the refuge has Dolly Varden.

Volcanic eruptions in 1977 formed Ukinrek Maars near the shore of Becharof Lake. For the first time, scientists were able to observe the creation of maars, steep-walled craters with little debris (i.e. cones) circling them. Maars are usually created by a one-time, water-rich, volcanic explosion. (S.E. Savage, USFWS)

Caribou range throughout the refuge, but the best time to look for them is in the fall and winter when the main herd migrates as far north as King Salmon. You never know about caribou though. They have been found on top of Mount Peulik in August, seeking escape from whitesocks by standing in the snowfields. They've also been spotted on beaches on the Pacific side for the same reason.

Moose are not as abundant, but they do browse up Big Creek, near the east end of

Lying along the Shelikof coast at the foot of Mount Becharof, Portage Bay is the site of the abandoned village of Kanatak. From there, Kanatak Pass leads to Island Arm of Becharof Lake. (Nina Faust)

Becharof Lake and in the Ruth River drainage.

Other recreational pursuits are beachcombing and clamming. Planes can land on beaches on the Pacific side at low tide, and every spring visitors head for razor and butter clam beds with shovel in hand.

Historians might like to pay Becharof a visit to view remnants of oil drilling at Puale Bay just after the turn of the century. Complete drilling rigs still stand, but remember, this is not a place for souvenir hunters.

Katmai National Park and Preserve

Recreation in Katmai can be summed up in three words: volcanoes, bears and fish. Most visitors fly in to Brooks Camp, on the shores of Naknek Lake and within a short walk of Brooks Lake. From there visitors can watch the big bruins which patrol the lakeshore, fish in Brooks River and occasionally take a shortcut right through camp. Fishermen need only take the trail to the river to compete with bears for a prize catch. (See Cautions, page 88, for etiquette and regulations for photographing and fishing near bears.) For another view of bears, and perhaps of a harlequin duck or two busy with its own fishing, walk to Brooks Falls. Or take the 4-mile trail to Dumpling Mountain for an overview of Naknek and Brooks lakes.

From Brooks Camp, a 23-mile road leads to the Valley of Ten Thousand Smokes. Katmailand staff run a van to the valley, where visitors can hike to the valley floor, or remain in the shelter

A short hike from Brooks Camp through the forest upriver toward Brooks Lake brings visitors to this bear-viewing platform overlooking Brooks Falls. Brown bears gather along the river to fish and waterfowl, such as mergansers and harlequins, can be seen patrolling the shoreline. (Kim Heacox)

*Visitors are drawn to Brooks Falls each summer to watch as
brown bears gather to feed on spawning salmon. (Kim Heacox)*

overlooking the ash-covered realm. Hikers can set out from there for extended trips deep into the mountains to Novarupta, heart of Katmai's cataclysmic eruption.

Canoeists might explore Savonoski Loop, a popular water route taking in Iliuk Arm and the Bay of Islands of Naknek Lake, Lake Grosvenor and the Grosvenor and Savonoski rivers. The rivers are safe for canoes but the braided channels may be difficult to follow. The trip takes five to 10 days, with a 1-mile portage between the Bay of Islands and Lake Grosvenor.

Rafters might consider running the Alagnak River, a portion of which is under the jurisdiction of the National Park Service as an officially designated wild river. Early season adventurers begin their float from Kukaklek Lake, the river's headwaters. A canyon downriver with Class III rapids in spots makes this route more challenging than departing from Nonvianuk Lake and following Nonvianuk River west until it joins with the Alagnak. The Alagnak runs about 80 miles before dumping into the Kvichak River, although tidal influences and power boats prompt most rafters to leave the river well before it reaches the Kvichak. The upper Alagnak is recommended for rafts only; canoes, kayaks and rafts are suitable for the Nonvianuk.

Harry Brod pedals his mountain bike along the road from Brooks Camp to the Valley of Ten Thousand Smokes. The road skirts hillsides and follows a river valley before climbing up to the overlook above Katmai's famous ash-covered valley.
(John Fowler)

The campground at Brooks Camp on Naknek Lake has three shelters to help campers get out of frequent summer showers.
(George Wuerthner)

This shelter, not always crowned with a rainbow, greets hikers who explore Baked Mountain. (Bud Rice)

Katmai is known for its fishing, with five species of salmon, rainbow and lake trout, Dolly Varden and arctic char, and arctic grayling and northern pike available in season in appropriate habitat. Brooks River receives by far the most visitor use, and as of June 1988 fishermen were allowed to keep one fish per day only. All other fishing is catch and release. The proximity of bears, fish and humans along the river has made this regulation necessary to maintain the special quality of the Brooks River experience.

Hunting is prohibited within the park, but is allowed in the preserve under State of Alaska regulations. Most hunters seek moose and caribou; trappers go for wolf, lynx and other furbearers.

McNeil River State Game Sanctuary

This sanctuary was set aside for the brown bears and photographing the bruins at close range provides the main recreational interest. See "McNeil River: Where the Bears Come First," page 65, for a description of the McNeil experience.

A camper pitches his tent on a bed of grass and cow parsnips on Takli Island, at the entrance to Amalik Bay. (Bud Rice)

Outdoor enthusiasts gather at this camp at Nonvianuk Lake. River runners can set out from here to raft the Nonvianuk and Alagnak rivers. (Steve McCutcheon)

Stacy Studebaker holds a string of black rock fish taken from Geographic Harbor. (Bud Rice)

A hiker is dwarfed by accumulated ash in the Valley of Ten Thousand Smokes. (Sean Reid)

A line of photographers focuses on a brown bear, the main draw at McNeil River State Game Sanctuary. (John Warden)

McNeil River: Where the Bears Come First

By Bill Sherwonit

Editor's note: Currently outdoors writer for the Anchorage Times, *Bill enjoys spending time at McNeil River, and has written several articles on the sanctuary.*

The bears have always come first at McNeil River State Game Sanctuary.

Created in 1967 by the Alaska Legislature, the sanctuary is intended, above all else, to protect one of the world's largest concentrations of brown bears.

The focal point of the gathering is McNeil Falls, where bears come each summer to feed on chum salmon returning to spawn. Typically they begin arriving at the falls in late June or early July and remain in large numbers until mid- to late August.

Last summer, state biologists identified 78 adult individuals at the falls. Including cubs, as many as 66 bears have been observed along the river at one time; and in 1986, 106 different bears were counted during one 24-hour period.

By nature, brown bears (the coastal counterparts of grizzlies) are solitary creatures. For them to gather in such large numbers — and in such close quarters — is exceptional.

During the past two decades, the Alaska Department of Fish and Game (ADF&G) has enacted a series of restrictions to ensure that this unique concentration is not disrupted by conflicts with humans.

Hunting and trapping are prohibited within the sanctuary, which is located at the northern end of the Alaska Peninsula just north of Katmai National Park and Preserve. All other human use is allowed "only to the extent that it does not significantly alter the bears' normal behavior." The McNeil River Brown Bear Management Plan further emphasizes that observation of brown bears should be the sanctuary's number one human use. And a limited-permit system has been established to regulate the number of people who watch and photograph the bears.

Two decades ago, McNeil River was virtually unknown as a bear-viewing site. Jim Faro, a state game biologist who managed the sanctuary at that time, recalls visitation was "very light in 1969. I think we had a total of six visitors the entire summer."

McNeil River State Game Sanctuary attracts photographers hoping for an opportunity to take that once-in-a-lifetime bear photo. (David Rhode)

Visitors to McNeil River stay in tents; the building in the background serves as cook shack, eating quarters and storage shed. (Bill Sherwonit)

By 1970, however, the media had begun to bring McNeil to the public's attention. Visitation, says Faro, was "distinctly up." And because there were no rules to regulate public use, human activities got out of control.

"We had people running up and down both sides of the river," Faro recalls. "There were even people fishing for salmon right at the falls where the bears feed. If all the horror stories you heard about bears are true, we should have had lots of dead people."

Instead, the bears went into hiding. "It was like the bears were saying, 'We don't have to put up with this.' They took one look at all the people and left," Faro says. Only a handful of bears remained.

During the same summer, a bear was killed by one of the sanctuary visitors. A photographer/guide decided to take some close-up pictures of a sow with cubs as the bears fed on the coastal mudflats. Crawling on hands and knees, he began his approach. The adult bear saw the movement and charged. Faro guesses the sow "probably thought he was another bear."

The bear came more than 100 yards across the flats. Expecting a false charge, the photographer remained on his hands and knees, rather than standing and identifying himself as a human. Finally, when the sow was only 60 to 70 feet away, the man made his move: He shot the bear with a .44 pistol. On being hit, the bear turned and fled. Unfortunately, she had been shot fatally in the lungs.

"The killing was totally unnecessary," Faro says. "It never should have happened."

It was obvious to Faro that tighter controls were needed, both to prevent future injurious encounters between bears and humans and to bring the bears back to McNeil Falls in large numbers. Finally, in 1973, the Alaska Board of Game approved a series of departmental proposals intended to restrict and regulate the activities of visitors to McNeil sanctuary during the prime-time bear-viewing period in July and August.

For the past 15 years, the state's primary control has been a permit system that limits viewing/ photography opportunities. From July 1 to August 25, no more than 10 people per day are allowed to visit McNeil Falls, and only while accompanied by one or two state biologists (who are outfitted with firearms).

The permit system has been highly successful. Since the state enacted its visitor restrictions, the number of bears visiting the falls has steadily increased.

Numbers tell only part of the story, however. Just as remarkable, if not more so, is the nature of human-bear interactions at McNeil. Since 1973, no bears have been killed in defense-of-life-or-property situations and no humans have been injured by bears. This, despite thousands of human-bear encounters, often at close range.

"It's widely assumed that bears and people don't mix," says Larry Aumiller, who has managed the sanctuary since the mid-1970s. "But here we've shown that they can mix, if you do the right things. To me, that's the most important message of McNeil: Humans can coexist with bears. It's an example of what could be."

Wildlife viewers and photographers set up their gear on a bluff above Mikfik Creek, in McNeil River State Game Sanctuary. The creek has recently become a popular spot for watching bears. (Bill Sherwonit)

Peaceful coexistence of humans and bears is possible because of a simple fact: McNeil bears are habituated to humans, but view them as neutral objects. People do not pose a threat. Neither are they a source of food.

To prevent any such association, feeding of bears is forbidden at McNeil (as it is throughout Alaska). Furthermore, a designated wood-frame building is provided for food storage, cooking and eating. And a no-bears-allowed policy is strictly enforced within a well-defined campground area.

Normally, bear "trespass" within the campground is not a problem. But occasionally a local resident — usually an adolescent bear — has to be taught the campground is off limits.

The education takes place in stages. Stage One is usually limited to loud, aggressive yelling. If yelling doesn't work, "we step it up a notch," Aumiller says. That next step involves the use of a "shell cracker," fired from a gun in the general direction of the bear and giving off a loud bang much like a firecracker. If there's still a problem, rubber pellets or even bird shot are used. But only rarely has Aumiller had to go as far as Stage Three.

Aumiller's education of McNeil bears goes beyond campground discipline, however. Through the years, he's made it easier for the bears to "read" people. The close supervision of sanctuary visitors is, in part, intended to make humans more predictable creatures.

Visitors to McNeil Falls are permitted to watch and photograph bears from a single, defined viewing area; only 10 per day are allowed at the falls; and viewing is done from late morning through early evening. Such routines and restrictions have made it easier for McNeil's bears to adapt to the "strange, hairless bipeds" (as Aumiller sometimes humorously refers to humans) who visit the falls during July and August. As a result, the bears have grown increasingly tolerant of people.

"In part, it's because we've fine-tuned our system," Aumiller says. "Plus the system has been in place now for 15 years. So young bears

Larry and Colleen Aumiller relax in their cabin at McNeil River, where Larry has been sanctuary manager since the mid-1970s. (Bill Sherwonit)

that grew up around humans are now grown up themselves and producing cubs of their own. We're to the second generation or beyond. There may have been as many bears around in the past; they just weren't as tolerant. Now we have bears doing things much more closely [to visitors], even sows nursing cubs."

Bears aren't the only ones to receive an education at McNeil. This is a valuable learning ground for humans as well.

Many visitors come to McNeil filled with irrational fears born of ignorance or sensationalized accounts of bear attacks. They carry the simplistic and inaccurate image of bears as menacing, dangerous creatures — unpredictable killers lurking in the shadows and waiting to attack.

McNeil helps to change such misconceptions. Visitors discover first-hand that bears aren't man-eating monsters as so often portrayed in literature and news accounts.

Says Aumiller, "The first day people come here, many of them are fearful, usually because of things they've heard or read. But after they've seen a few bears up close and the bears go about their business, people get incredibly blasé about it. After that, we have to caution them about getting too careless. The transformation is almost universal."

Aumiller believes McNeil's visitors feel safe around the bears largely because the sanctuary provides a controlled situation. The biologists act as guides. And they're armed, although they've never had to shoot a bear. Also, Aumiller notes, "McNeil is a well-known place. People are aware there haven't been any attacks since we've been using the permit system."

The removal of irrational fears makes it easier to accept the bears on their own terms. And as professional wildlife photographer Wayne Lynch has noted, there is no better place than McNeil to see "bears acting as bears."

"In most places, you see bears in transition. Here, you get a glimpse of their lives," Lynch says. "You come to see them as the individuals they are, to empathize with them."

The ability to perceive bears as individuals is enhanced by Fish and Game's bear-naming system. All adult bears that visit McNeil Falls on a regular basis are given names: Melody, Weird, Romeo, Chaser, Groucho and Flashman are examples. (Adolescents are known simply as Norton.) Though such naming might be criticized by some wildlife biologists, there is, in fact, a scientific justification for the system: Names make it easier to keep track of individuals. And no one has been able to come up with a better identification system since radio-collars and tags were banned in the 1970s because they detracted from McNeil's primary use as a viewing/photography area.

Until the mid-1980s, few people visited McNeil sanctuary before July 1. With no concentrations of bears to see, there was little reason to. But in 1982, a new pattern began to emerge, because of changes at a neighboring stream of McNeil River named Mikfik Creek.

Mikfik is a small, clearwater creek that flows through the sanctuary and enters a saltwater lagoon less than a mile from McNeil River. It hosts a run of sockeye salmon during mid- to late June, but historically the run has been so small — a few thousand fish — that bears largely ignored the salmon.

Then, for reasons biologists can only guess, Mikfik's sockeye return began to increase dramatically in size. Over the past seven years, the creek's salmon run has ranged from a low of 12,800 fish in 1983 to a high of 87,000 in 1985.

Not surprisingly, increasing numbers of bears have been attracted to Mikfik's improved fishing opportunities. And

nobody visited the sanctuary in June," Sellers says. But in 1988, the June visitor count was 70 people.

If such early-season visitation continues to increase, the state will likely expand its permit system to include all or part of June. But for 1989, at least, sanctuary visitors will be allowed to view bears at Mikfik Creek on a first-come, first-served basis. Even in June, the 10-viewer limit is strictly enforced when visiting the bears' fishing ground.

Brown bears aren't the only users drawn to Mikfik's sockeye runs, however. Commercial seiners have harvested the creek's salmon for decades, but only since 1982 has the run attracted major attention. As the return increased, so did fishing pressure.

In recent years, ADF&G game biologists have recognized an increased potential for conflict between the commercial fishery and

following closely behind are bear watchers and photographers.

"Previously there might have been three or four bears fishing Mikfik Creek in June. Now we're getting up to 20 bears there," says Dick Sellers, a game biologist whose management area includes McNeil sanctuary.

Visitor numbers have jumped even more dramatically. As recently as five or six years ago, "virtually sanctuary values. At times there has been considerable tension between the department's Game and Commercial Fish divisions. But state biologists have worked out a truce that allows restricted, supervised seining within the sanctuary boundaries when sockeye escapement goals have been met.

Such commercial fishing will be permitted in the foreseeable future, but only as long as it doesn't interfere with McNeil's unique gathering of bears.

How to Visit McNeil

Permits to visit McNeil River State Game Sanctuary during the prime-time viewing period from July 1 to August 25 are issued through a lottery that is held each April 15.

Applications are due in the Anchorage ADF&G office by April 1 and must be accompanied by $50 for each person listed on the application form. Ten dollars of that total is a non-refundable application fee; the remainder is a sanctuary use fee. Unsuccessful applicants will receive a $40 refund following the drawing. Drawing winners may return their permits no later than June 1 for a refund of the use fee, if unable to visit the sanctuary.

The department has developed a standby system to fill vacancies created when lottery winners fail to use their permits. Standby visitors are not assured of visiting McNeil Falls, but over the past few years increasing numbers of people have been willing to take that gamble and the sanctuary campground has at times become overcrowded. Beginning in 1988, the Department of Fish and Game began charging all standby visitors a use fee of $25 — without any guarantees of getting to the falls. Those planning to visit McNeil on a standby basis are advised to check with Fish and Game to see if any vacancies exist and get some idea of how much "competition" they can expect.

Access to the sanctuary is primarily by air. Most visitors use air charter services based in Homer, King Salmon or Anchorage. State policies prevent Fish and Game from recommending any specific private charter operators, but the department will provide a list of licensed air carriers upon request if a self-addressed, stamped envelope is included.

McNeil River visitors must be entirely self-sufficient and prepared for a wilderness experience; no commercial facilities are available. Even in summer, equipment and clothing must be adequate to withstand cold and wet weather. Visitors are also cautioned that bad weather can prevent departure for several days.

Application forms and further information on the McNeil sanctuary can be obtained by writing to the Alaska Department of Fish and Game, Game Division, 333 Raspberry Road, Anchorage, AK 99518.

Communities

Today residents of Katmai country concentrate in four communities: Naknek, South Naknek and King Salmon along the Naknek River and at the river's outlet into Kvichak Bay; and Egegik, on the region's west coast at the mouth of the Egegik River. Outside these towns, only scattered homesites and homesteaders' cabins dot the countryside. In years past, Natives gathered in a few other villages, but these have been abandoned for decades.

A 15-mile road, built by the Army Corps of Engineers in 1949, connects inland King Salmon to Naknek on the coast. No roads reach South Naknek, across the river. Although the population of Naknek and South Naknek swells to several thousand during the summer fishing season, the year-round count at Naknek is about 300, at South Naknek about 180.

King Salmon, whose economy depends more on government services than on fishing, has an unofficial population of more than 500, but this includes about 300 personnel stationed at King Salmon Air Force Base. Originally an air navigation site, the station became an Air Force base at the beginning of World War II. The military facility is one of two forward operating bases for the Air Force in western Alaska. The other is at Galena. The 21st Tactical Fighter Wing has two F15s on 24-hour alert at King Salmon to intercept foreign planes and escort them away from U.S. air space.

Egegik, 40 miles south of King Salmon, was built around a cannery in the early 1900s, and today the community still depends on commercial fishing. Egegik's winter population

Cannery buildings and fishing boats dominate this view of Egegik, a village on the northwest coast of the Alaska Peninsula. Egegik's winter population, about 100, grows to 1,000 to 3,000 in summer. (David Rhode)

Domestic fowl lining a fence at Naknek contribute to the rural atmosphere. (Alissa Crandall)

The community of King Salmon began as an air navigation site, then became an air force base at the beginning of World War II. The photo above shows base living quarters in 1952. At left, students are all smiles in their modern classroom in 1961. (Both, FAA Collection, Anchorage Museum)

An apartment building is under construction in Naknek in 1949. The town began as and remains a major center for commercial fishing and processing. (FAA Collection, Anchorage Museum)

of about 100 increases by 10 to 30 times during the busy summer fishing season. Several area canneries provide seasonal jobs, and residents supplement this income with subsistence hunting and fishing. Egegik is accessible only by air or boat.

Most passengers and freight reach Katmai country through the air transportation hub at King Salmon, although barge service operates into Naknek between May and October. Severe tidal changes, up to 18 feet, limit boat traffic on the Naknek River beyond South Naknek to vessels drawing 4 feet or less. Some fishermen take their boats around the Alaska Peninsula, through a pass in the Aleutians and up into Bristol Bay to a dock along the Kvichak coast or in the Naknek River. When ice covers the river, the waterway is sometimes used for travel between King Salmon and Naknek.

Ever since the first fish processing plant opened on the Naknek River in 1890, salmon

The community of South Naknek stretches out along the south shore of the Naknek River. (Jim Simmen)

runs have nourished the region's economy. And being at the heart of the world's largest red salmon runs hasn't hurt. Fishing boats swarm in Bristol Bay, bringing part of their catch to processors at Naknek. English is just one of many languages heard among chattering crews at the canneries where most employees come from outside the region. Returning king salmon reach the region in late May, reds predominate in June and July, followed by silver, pink and chum in the fall. Between 4,000 and 5,000 are employed in the fishing industry at the season's peak. In addition to salmon, a few boats fish for herring off Togiak.

After the frenzy of the commercial fishing season, residents settle down to government, retail and service jobs, and subsistence hunting and fishing. Recreation centers on making the most of the area's natural resources. Sport fishing for freshwater species goes on year-round. A short drive out from King Salmon and just within the national park boundary lies Lake Camp, a good spot to put in a boat and head up Naknek Lake. Sport fishermen can try their luck here as late as October. In the fall, hunters seek caribou, moose and bear. Caribou from the Alaska Peninsula herd cross the road to Lake Camp in October. The area is not known for good moose hunting, although these animals browse in stream drainages flowing into the Naknek.

A good supply of furbearers tempt trappers each winter. Fox, beaver, otter, lynx and wolf skins bring extra cash.

In summer, air taxis are busy taking visitors into Katmai and Becharof backcountry. Tourists keep up a steady stream of traffic through King Salmon to Brooks Camp and the Valley of Ten Thousand Smokes in the national park through mid-September. King Salmon has several lodges set up to cater to visiting fishermen and hunters.

Fish canneries, mainstay of the economy, line the shore at the village of Naknek. (Steve McCutcheon)

King Salmon sprawls along the bank of the Naknek River. A majority of the community's residents work at the King Salmon Air Force Base. (Steve McCutcheon)

Subsistence fishermen Frank Schroder and Ann Shankle of King Salmon pick red salmon from their net on the Naknek River. (Jim Simmen)

Trapper Billy Nekeferoff, a longtime resident of Katmai country, poses with stretched beaver pelts along Becharof Lake in this 1979 photo. (David Rhode)

Naknek, however, has more year-round commercial outlets.

Several schools provide an education for the region's children. Egegik's school spans kindergarten through 8th grade; children from King Salmon are bused to elementary and high school in Naknek. Students from South Naknek attend elementary school in their own village, but are flown across the river every weekday to attend high school at Naknek. Medical facilities are located in Naknek, as are the offices of Bristol Bay Borough, established in 1962 as the first borough in the state. Egegik has a small clinic and one nearby lodge, but offers few other services, particularly in winter.

For most year-round residents, the grandeur of their mountain-flanked surroundings and supreme fishing more than offset the isolation and limited exposure to the urban lifestyle that goes with living in Katmai country.

John and Bill Knutsen check their mink traps along Peters Creek, near Naknek. (Alissa Crandall)

The Ukak River cuts through the blanket of ash in the Valley of Ten Thousand Smokes in Katmai National Park. The 5,010-foot mountain in the background honors Rolf Werner Juhle, who drowned in Knife Creek in 1953. (Charles Kay)

How To Get There

By far the majority of visitors to Katmai National Park and Preserve, McNeil River State Game Sanctuary and Becharof National Wildlife Refuge arrive by plane. King Salmon is the transfer hub, with major commercial flights connecting with bush flights to outlying communities, backcountry lodges and drop-off points. A jet flight from Anchorage takes about 50 minutes; two hours if the flight goes through Dillingham.

Visitors to McNeil and the Cook Inlet/Shelikof Strait side of Katmai usually fly out of Homer; those heading for Becharof leave from Kodiak.

If you have access to a boat, you can reach the area by water. The Pacific coast is extremely rugged, however, and seldom do casual visitors arrive in this fashion. The trip around the Alaska Peninsula to the Bering Sea coast is long and just as hazardous.

Once at King Salmon, visitors can rent a vehicle and drive to Naknek, or drive in the opposite direction to Lake Camp, at the outlet of Naknek Lake. Bush flights go to Brooks Camp, or several other lodges within Katmai country.

Becharof National Wildlife Refuge is more remote, and getting there can be half the fun. Air taxis on floats can land on Becharof Lake, or on lakes in the Kejulik River valley. Numerous sand bars and sand blows on which small planes on wheels can land are scattered throughout the refuge. There is also a landing strip, originally put in by oil companies, south of the refuge at Wide Bay on the Pacific side. Air taxis can also take visitors to Egegik, from where travelers can

A floatplane from Homer unloads its passengers and cargo at McNeil River. (John Warden)

To avoid attracting bears, food and trash at Brooks Camp is stored out of harm's way in this cache. (Sean Reid)

Brooks Lodge, one of six lodges in Katmai National Park and Preserve, is nestled among the trees on the Brooks River.
(Alissa Crandall)

upstream on Big Creek, a tributary of the Naknek River.

Where To Stay

Katmai National Park and Preserve has six lodges and one maintained campground, that on the shores of Naknek Lake near Brooks Camp. There are 21 campsites, three with three-sided wooden shelters to protect gear somewhat from frequent summer rains. Campground capacity is 60 campers, limited to 7 days per stay. Campsites are assigned by reservation. All other accommodations at Katmai are under the stars or the tent you carry with you. All backcountry users must have a valid backcountry permit, obtainable at no charge from Park Service staff.

Becharof has no lodges or maintained campgrounds. All visitors to McNeil must stay in the one maintained campground.

King Salmon has several lodges and hotels, and Egegik has a lodge.

Services

Services within Katmai center at Brooks Camp where Katmailand operates a lodge under contract with the Park Service. Guests stay in cabins and take their meals in the main lodge. There is also a small trading post there. Park Service staff maintain a ranger station and visitor center, with guided nature walks and

boat up the Egegik River 10 miles to Becharof Lake. It is also possible to hike in from Egegik, but in the words of refuge manager Ron Hood, this is "major league adventure" because of heavy marshes along the hiking route. Jet boats can reach the edge of the refuge by going

The Valley of Ten Thousand Smokes offers little shelter for campers, as is shown by this bleak campsite near Novarupta. (Chlaus Lotscher)

Weather in Katmai country can be as hazardous as it is unpredictable. Windstorms are common in the Valley of Ten Thousand Smokes, where windblown ash can make visibility impossible. On Naknek and other area lakes, winds can be a hazard and boaters are advised to stay close to shore.
(Left, Sean Reid; above, Karen Jettmar)

for guests of the lodges or for guests of commercial-use licensees outside the park who bring in visitors, chiefly sport fishermen, for one-day trips.

Cautions

Big bears rule Katmai country and visitors must at all times remember that bears have the right-of-way. Park Service staff insist that visitors stay 50 yards from bears — 100 yards from sows with cubs. At all times, back off a trail or beach to let a bear pass. If you should encounter a bear, back slowly away, do not run. When hiking in brush, make noise to alert the bear of your presence.

Discourage any bear from associating humans with food. If camping, store and cook all food away from your tent. Eliminate all highly odoriferous items from your gear. If you are fishing when a bear comes by, do your best to prevent any link between you and the fish in the bear's mind.

Once you have the bear etiquette down, remember that traveling anywhere in Alaska's backcountry requires certain precautions. In Katmai country, be prepared for wind and rain. Winds exceeding 50 miles per hour can rush

visitor programs in the evenings.

Katmailand also operates van service to the Valley of Ten Thousand Smokes. Cost in 1988 was $56 round trip.

Other services within Katmai are available

down the valleys, collapsing poorly anchored tents. In the Valley of Ten Thousand Smokes, wind-blown ash can cut visibility to zero. Do not travel in poor visibility, especially if you have to ford rivers. Set up camp and wait.

Wind, combined with the moisture from frequent summer rains, can draw away your body heat and cause hypothermia. And dehydration can sap your strength. Rains can also cause rivers to swell, blocking your advance or retreat. Again, stay dry and wait out the storm. When conditions are right to cross the river, face upstream and angle slightly downstream. Keep a sturdy stick handy for balance, and loosen the straps on your pack in

Weather is not a new hazard in Katmai country, as shown by this October 2, 1949, view of the Naknek sea plane and scow landing beach, photographed during a "lull between 70-mile gusts." (FAA Collection, Anchorage Museum)

case you have to jettison it quickly. Try to cross in the morning when water levels are lower, and test for deep holes or for quicksand with your stick. Quicksand accumulates in eddies where two channels meet.

Now that you have the precautions in hand, head for Katmai country, where powerful brownies and sleek rainbows and sockeyes play in a world where the land shakes and the mountains grumble.

Bibliography

Bancroft, Hubert Howe. *History of Alaska 1730-1885.* New York: Antiquarian Press Ltd., 1970.

Bohn, Dave. *Rambles through an Alaskan Wild.* Santa Barbara, Calif.: Capra Press, 1979.

Clark, Gerald H. *Archaeology on the Alaska Peninsula: The Coast of Shelikof Strait 1963-1965.* University of Oregon Anthropological Papers, No. 13, 1977.

Colby, Merle. *A Guide to Alaska.* New York: The MacMillan Company, 1959.

Damas, David, ed. *Handbook of North American Indians.* Vol. 5, Arctic. Washington, D.C.: Smithsonian Institution, 1984.

Dumond, D.E. *A Summary of Archaeology in the Katmai Region, Southwestern Alaska.* University of Oregon Anthropological Papers, No. 2, 1971.

Erskine, William Fiske. *Katmai.* New York: Abelard-Schuman,1962.

Fierstein, Judy. *The Valley of Ten Thousand Smokes.* Anchorage: Alaska Natural History Association, 1984.

Griggs, Robert F. *The Valley of Ten Thousand Smokes.* Washington, D.C.: The National Geographic Society, 1922.

John Fowler studies the ash fall that covered much of the Valley of Ten Thousand Smokes during the 1912 eruption of Novarupta Volcano. (Courtesy of John Fowler)

Johnson, Susan Hackley, ed. *Exploring Katmai National Monument and the Valley of Ten Thousand Smokes.* Anchorage: Alaska Travel Publications, Inc., 1974.

Martin, George C. "The Recent Eruption of Katmai Volcano in Alaska." *National Geographic* 24 (2), 1913: pages 131-181.

Pierce, Richard A., ed. *The Russian Orthodox Religious Mission in America, 1794-1837.* Materials for the Study of Alaska History, No. 11. Kingston, Ontario: The Limestone Press, 1978.

—*Siberia and Northwestern America 1788-1792.* Materials for the Study of Alaska History, No. 17. Kingston, Ontario: The Limestone Press, 1980.

U.S. Department of the Interior, Fish and Wildlife Service. *Becharof National Wildlife Refuge: Draft Wilderness Review Amendment and Supplemental Environmental Impact Statement.* Anchorage, July 1988.

U.S. Department of the Interior, National Park Service. *Draft Environmental Impact Statement for the Wilderness Recommendation: Katmai National Park and Preserve.* Washington, D.C.: U.S. Government Printing Office, 1988.

—*Draft General Management Plan/Environmental Assessment, Land Protection Plan, Wilderness Suitability Review: Katmai National Park and Preserve.* Washington, D.C.: U.S. Government Printing Office, 1985.

Index

Alaska Geographic® Back Issues

The North Slope, Vol. 1, No. 1. Charter issue. *Out of print.*

One Man's Wilderness, Vol. 1, No. 2. *Out of print.* (Book edition available, $19.95)

Admiralty...Island in Contention, Vol. 1, No. 3. In-depth review of Southeast's Admiralty Island. 78 pages, $5.

Fisheries of the North Pacific: History, Species, Gear & Processes, Vol. 1, No.4. *Out of Print.* (Book edition available, $24.95.)

The Alaska-Yukon Wild Flowers Guide, Vol. 2, No. 1. *Out of print.* (Book edition available, $12.95)

Richard Harrington's Yukon, Vol .2, No. 2. *Out of print.*

Prince William Sound, Vol. 2, No. 3. *Out of print.*

Yakutat: The Turbulent Crescent, Vol. 2, No. 4. *Out of print.*

Glacier Bay: Old Ice, New Land, Vol. 3, No. 1. *Out of print.*

The Land: Eye of the Storm, Vol. 3, No. 2. *Out of print.*

Richard Harrington's Antarctic, Vol. 3, No. 3. Reviews Antarctica and islands of southern polar regions, territories of mystery and controversy. Fold-out map. 104 pages, $8.95.

The Silver Years of the Alaska Canned Salmon Industry: An Album of Historical Photos, Vol. 3, No. 4. *Out of print.*

Alaska's Volcanoes: Northern Link in the Ring of Fire, Vol. 4 No. 1. *Out of print.*

The Brooks Range: Environmental Watershed, Vol. 4, No. 2. *Out of print.*

Kodiak: Island of Change, Vol. 4, No. 3. *Out of print.*

Wilderness Proposals: Which Way for Alaska's Lands?, Vol. 4, No. 4. *Out of print.*

Cook Inlet Country, Vol. 5, No. 1. *Out of print.*

Southeast: Alaska's Panhandle, Vol. 5, No. 2. Explores southeastern Alaska's maze of fjords and islands, forests and mountains, from Dixon Entrance to Icy Bay, including all of the Inside Passsage. The book profiles every town, and reviews the region's history, economy, people, attractions and future. fold-out map. 192 pages, $12.95.

Bristol Bay Basin, Vol. 5, No. 3. *Out of print.*

Alaska Whales and Whaling, Vol. 5, No. 4. The wonders of whales in Alaska — their life cycles, travels and travails — are examined, with an authoritative history of commercial and subsistence whaling in the North. Includes a fold-out poster of 14 major whale species in Alaska in perspective, color photos and illustrations, with historical photos and line drawings. 144 pages, $19.95.

Yukon-Kuskokwim Delta, Vol. 6, No. 1. *Out of print.*

The Aurora Borealis, Vol. 6, No. 2. Explores the northern lights in history and today; their cause, how they work, and their importance in contemporary science. 96 pages, $7.95.

Alaska's Native People, Vol. 6, No. 3. Examines the worlds of the Inupiat and Yupik Eskimo, Athabascan, Aleut, Tlingit, Haida and Tsimshian. Fold-out map of Native villages and language areas. 304 pages, $24.95.

The Stikine River, Vol. 6, No. 4. River route to three Canadian gold strikes, the Stikine is the largest and most navigable of several rivers that flow from northwestern Canada through southeastern Alaska to the Pacific Ocean. Fold-out map. 96 pages. $9.95.

Alaska's Great Interior, Vol. 7, No.1. Examines the people, communities, economy, and wilderness of Alaska's rich Interior, the immense valley between the Alaska Range and Brooks Range. Fold-out map. 128 pages, $9.95.

A Photographic Geography of Alaska, Vol. 7, No. 2. A visual tour through the six regions of Alaska: Southeast, Southcentral/ Gulf Coast, Alaska Peninsula and Aleutians, Bering Sea Coast, Arctic and Interior. 192 pages, $15.95.

The Aleutians, Vol. 7, No. 3. Home of the Aleut, a tremendous wildlife spectacle, a major World War II battleground, and an important arm of Alaska's commercial fishing industry. Fold-out map. 224 pages, $14.95.

Klondike Lost: A Decade of Photographs by Kinsey & Kinsey, Vol. 7, No. 4. Out of print. (Book edition available, $12.95.)

Wrangell-Saint Elias, Vol. 8, No. 1. Alaska's only designated World Heritage Area, this mountain wilderness takes in the nation's largest national park in its sweep from the Copper River across the Wrangell Mountains to the southern tip of the Saint Elias Range near Yakutat. Fold-out map. 144 pages, $19.95.

Alaska Mammals, Vol. 8, No. 2. Reviews in anecdotes and facts the entire spectrum of Alaska's wildlife. 184 pages, $12.95.

The Kotzebue Basin, Vol. 8, No. 3. Examines northwestern Alaska's thriving trading area of Kotzebue Sound and the Kobuk and Noatak river basins. 184 pages, $12.95.

Alaska National Interest Lands, Vol. 8, No. 4. Reviews each of Alaska's national interest land (d-2 lands) selections, outlining location, size, access and briefly describes special attractions. 242 pages, $14.95.

Alaska's Glaciers, Vol. 9, No. 1. Examines in-depth the massive rivers of ice, their composition, exploration, present-day distribution and scientific significance. Illustrated with many comtemporary color and historical black-and-white photos, the text includes separate discussions of more than a dozen glacial regions. 144 pages, $19.95.

Sitka and Its Ocean/Island World, Vol. 9, No. 2. From the elegant capital of Russian America to a beautiful but modern port, Sitka, on Baranof Island, has become a commercial and cultural center for Southeastern Alaska. 128 pages, $19.95.

Islands of the Sealsa; The Pribilofs, Vol. 9, No. 3. Great herds of northern fur seals and immense flocks of seabirds share their island homeland with Aleuts brought to this remote Bering Sea outpost by Russians. 128 pages, $9.95.

Alaska's Oil/Gas & Minerals Industry, Vol. 9, No. 4. Experts detail the geological processes and resulting mineral and fossil fuel resources that contribute substantially to Alaska's economy. 216 pages, $12.95.

Adventure Roads North: The Story of the Alaska Highway and Other Roads in *The MILEPOST®*. Vol. 10, No.1. Reviews the history of Alaska's roads and takes a mile-by-mile look at the country they cross. 224 pages, $14.95.

Anchorage and the Cook Inlet Basin, Vol. 10, No. 2. Reviews in-depth the commercial and urban center of the Last Frontier. Three fold-out maps. 168 pages, $14.95.

Alaska's Salmon Fisheries, Vol. 10, No. 3. A comprehensive look at Alaska's most valuable commercial fishery. 128 pages. $12.95.

Up the Koyukuk, Vol. 10, No. 4. Highlights the wildlife and traditional native lifestyle of this remote region of northcentral Alaska. 152 pages. $14.95.

Nome: City of the Golden Beaches, Vol. 11, No. 1. Reviews the colorful history of one of Alaska's most famous gold rush towns. 184 pages, $14.95.

Alaska's Farms and Gardens, Vol. 11, No. 2. An overview of the past, present and future of agriculture in Alaska, with details on growing your own vegetables in the North. 144 pages, $12.95.

Chilkat River Valley, Vol. 11, No. 3. Explores the mountain-rimmed valley at the head of the Inside Passage, its natural resources, and the residents who have settled there. 112 pages, $12.95.

Alaska Steam, Vol. 11, No. 4. Pictorial history of the pioneering Alaska Steamship Company. 160 pages. $12.95.

Northwest Territories, Vol. 12, No. 1. In-depth look at the magnificent wilderness of Canada's high Arctic. Fold-out map. 136 pages, $12.95.

Alaska's Forest Resources, Vol. 12, No. 2. Examines the botanical, recreational and economic value of Alaska's forests. 200 pages, $14.95.

Alaska Native Arts and Crafts, Vol. 12, No. 3. In-depth review of the art and artifacts of Alaska's Natives. 215 pages, $17.95.

Our Arctic Year, Vol. 12, No. 4. Compelling story of a year in the wilds of the Brooks Range. 150 pages, $12.95.

Where Mountains Meet the Sea: Alaska's Gulf Coast, Vol. 13, No. 1. Alaskan's first-hand descriptions of the 850-mile arc that crowns the Pacific Ocean from Kodiak to Cape Spencer at the entrance to southeastern Alaska's Inside Passage. 191 pages, $14.95.

Backcountry Alaska, Vol. 13, No. 2. A full-color look at the remote communities of Alaska. Companion volume to The *ALASKA WILDERNESS MILEPOST®.* 224 pages, $14.95.

British Columbia's Coast/The Canadian Inside Passage, Vol. 13, No. 3. Reviews the B.C. coast west of the Coast Mountain divide from mighty Vancouver and elegant Victoria in the south, to the forested wilderness to the north, including the Queen Charlotte islands. Fold-out map. 200 pages, $14.95.

Lake Clark/Lake Iliamna Country, Vol. 13, No. 4. Chronicles the human and natural history of the region that many claim has a sampling of all the best that Alaska has to offer in natural beauty. 152 pages, $14.95.

Dogs of the North, Vol. 14, No. 1. The first men to cross the Bering Land Bridge probably brought dogs to Alaska. This issue examines the development of northern breeds from the powerful husky and malemute to the fearless little Tahltan bear dog, the evolution of the dogsled, uses of dogs, and the history of sled-dog racing from the All-Alaska Sweepstakes of 1908 to the nationally televised Iditarod of today. 120 pages, $16.95.

South/Southeast Alaska, Vol. 14, No. 2. Reviews the natural and human resources of the southernmost tip of Alaska's Panhandle, from Sumner Strait to the Canadian border. Fold-out map. 120 pages, $14.95.

Alaska's Seward Peninsula, Vol. 14, No. 3. The Seward Peninsula is today's remnant of the Bering Land Bridge, gateway to an ancient America. This issue chronicles the blending of traditional Eskimo culture with the white man's persistent search for gold. Fold-out map. 112 pages, $14.95.

The Upper Yukon Basin, Vol. 14, No. 4. Yukoner Monty Alford describes this remote region, headwaters for one of the continent's mightiest rivers and gateway for some of Alaska's earliest pioneers. 117 pages, $14.95.

Glacier Bay: Icy Wilderness, Vol. 15, No. 1. Covers the 5,000-square-mile wilderness now known as Glacier Bay National Park and Preserve, including the natural and human history of the Glacier Bay area, its wildlife, how to get there, what to expect, and what changes now seem predictable. 103 pages, $14.95.

Dawson City, Vol. 15, No. 2. For two years just before the turn of the century, writes author Mike Doogan, news from Dawson City blazed like a nova around the world and a million people wanted to go there. Like a nova, the gold rush burned out quickly, but its light still illuminates the city it built. In this issue Doogan examines the geology and the history of the Klondike, and why a million tourists want to go to Dawson while other gold-rush towns of the North are only collapsed cabins and faded memories. 94 pages, historic and contemporary photos, index, $14.95.

Denali, Vol. 15, No. 3. It was *Denali* to the Tanana Indians, *Doleika,* to the nearby Tanainas, *Bolshaya Gora* to the Russians, all connoting size and height and scenic grandeur. A gold-prospector called it *McKinley* less than a century ago, and unfortunately that name endured. But the mountain massif in southcentral Alaska, by whatever name, has fascinated man from the primitive to the present. This book is an in-depth guide to the Great One, its lofty neighbors and the surrounding wilderness now known as Denali National Park and Preserve. 94 pages, historic and contemporary photos, index, $14.95.

The Kuskokwim River, Vol. 15, No. 4. A review of one of Alaska's most important rivers, this issue focuses on the entire Kuskokwim drainage, from the headwaters to the mouth on Kuskokwim Bay. Author Mary Lenz discusses natural and human history along the river, including mining, fishing, riverboats and village life. 94 pages, historic and comtemporary photos, index, $14.95.

NEXT ISSUE:

North Slope Now, Vol. 16, No. 2. Much has changed on Alaska's northern fringe since our original issue was prepared on the North Slope: the trans-Alaska pipeline, vastly expanded oil development, major new mineral finds, the debate over the Arctic National Wildlife Refuge. This issue will remind readers of the isolated world north of the Brooks Range® and bring them up-to-date on the economic forces that have propelled the slope into the limelight. To members mid-year, 1989. Price to be announced.

ALL PRICES SUBJECT TO CHANGE.

Your $39 membership in The Alaska Geographic Society includes four subsequent issues of *ALASKA GEOGRAPHIC®,* the Society's official quarterly. Please add $4 for non-U.S. membership.

Additional membership information is available upon request. Single copies of the *ALASKA GEOGRAPHIC®* back issues are also available. When ordering, please make payments in U.S. funds and add $1.50 postage/handling per copy. To order back issues, send your check or money order and volumes desired to:

The Alaska Geographic Society

P.O. Box 93370, Anchorage, Alaska 99509